I0178059

The Quarter Life Crisis Poet

Dedicated to:
All the Love in the World

Also by Catherine Vaughan

Welcome to Wonderland

About the Author

Catherine Vaughan is a British Writer. With Dreams of Bohemia in her heart she does occasional poetry readings in quaint cafés and performed at Ledbury Poetry Festival and The Cheltenham Literature Festival. She enjoys writing poetry, short stories and novels. **"Welcome to Wonderland"** is her first novel and is Book 1 of a Bohemian Love Story.

The Quarter Life Crisis Poet:
A Collection of Poems on Pain, Heartbreak and Defiance by a Twenty-Something

Copyright © 2015 Catherine Vaughan

Published in the United Kingdom by Jolie Girl Publishing.
www.CatherineVaughan.com

Fifth Edition
ISBN: 978-0-9934-0890-8

The right of Catherine Vaughan to be identified as the author of this work has been asserted in accordance the Copyright, Designs and Patents Act of 1988

All rights reserved. No part of this book may be reproduced by any mechanical, photographic, or electronic process, or in the form of a phonographic recording, nor may it be stored in a retrieval system, transmitted, or otherwise be copied for public or private use- other than for "fair use" as brief quotations embodied in articles and reviews without prior written permission of the publisher.

The Quarter Life Crisis Poet

A Collection of Poems on Pain, Heartbreak and Defiance by a Twenty-Something.

CATHERINE VAUGHAN

CONTENTS

LOST GENERATION

We are the heir
To Blair
In academia we make our bet
They get into debt.

Fortune is linear?
Starve, charge, and never recharge.
Let's get skinnier.

We are living it up
Naivety of a pup
In the workplace we are like slaves
Then at night we rave.

Our big break will come.
Chase, trace, and encase.
To the beat of our drum

But I will not succumb

You are all so dumb
Here I become

And then some...

An artist.
I escaped to Bohemia

Away from academia
Ran from the curse
In my converse
And then some

Ran away from academia
Away from the curse
In my converse
To Bohemia

2am

I feel it in my chest, the grip of heartache.
He won't let me go.
His hold is tough on my love.
My heart aches from his unrelenting hold on my
heart
His hold on my body
I want you so bad I'll go back on the things I
believe
All the way to the edge of desire

Yet NO call
You expect my all
Under the sheets I see your face as if we were in
our intimacy
You only love with half
Of that dead beat inside you
I confess: I still wish we had our chance
We never had our dance
Never said to try
Again

So why are you breaking my heart
Over
And
Over
Again
?

CHASING YESTERDAY

The hurt has run a marathon
Going on for months, years and so it seems
by now
A decade
I've crashed and burned from it yet it still
perseveres.
Do you know you?
Backwards steps as the years pass

so I ran back to you… for the summer.

THE BEAST

Not another text
Aren't you already sexed?

I called you dummy
Still need your Mummy?

You want my body
I can disembody.

Newport, California, USA

I felt free, I discovered the land of
freedom.
Escaped this Capital. North Korea.
Seeped into the mind
Subtle design.

Why had it taken me so long to get
here?
There was the abuse, misuse
Of information
No liberation

Not about North Korea nor California
Can't you get what I mean?
You are green.

In the here and now
Hear you how?

e-mail
me.

I WANT TO BE INNOVATIVE

I am in this new world.
It's been here the whole time.
How could I have not noticed?
It is me, it is within me.
Freedom
Here at last?
Is it bollocks or is it Art?
Are they just telling us all lies?
I will be first!
Consumed with all that knowledge that
quenched my thirst.

BLONDE

I like being blonde
My world opened up when I had that
glimmer of sunlight streak through my
hair.
I met you and I loved you
I felt the freedom
Blondes do have more fun
My life got better
Sunshine beaming off me
I was radiant

Ennui.

It set in. The summer of my vision faded
away along with
It.

THAT FORGOTTEN ENEMY

It seeped into my life when I was a child
Mother made me look in the mirror
She forced me
Flaw after flaw
made me look at the floor.

I could never see any lightness in me
It was all dark dark
misery never left me.

Love was my cure
or so I thought.
I never felt enough of it
my nerves my nerves
too much happened.

But beauty rescued me
or so I thought
Beauty was another disguise for it
Obsession

Obsession
on my own no escape.

Up the stairs

That's when you first saw me
You wanted me from then on
Three years later

You & I at last
Love Love.

You comforted me,
held me close
you protected me from it.

When you left
It came back
Now I face the enemy in a different
Form. Anna with a silent 'n'.

DANCING WITH FEAR

Why do I dance with you?
Why do I stand next to you?
Why don't you ever leave me the way my True
Love left me?
Day and night I feel you there.
Will you please stop that stare.

Why do I let it linger and let it wear
me down?
What if in the here and now I had nothing to
worry about?
Yet why does this ego suck me into this anxiety?
This is what I need to

                        overcome.

Now I wonder why should I care?
Think you can hurt me? Don't you dare.
Now I need to rid of this drudging feeling.
It can't go on for you too.
I know what to do.

Choose the Path of Peace
Hold lightly on to every piece.
I know that I can release.
It has left my core.
Be gone - no more

But tell me why did they all leave her?
Why did they all watch on as she cried?
No comfort given her way
Just cold hard stares.

I'm still trying to get them,
to get friends.
Maybe just a friend.
A boyfriend? Well, I had a
non-boyfriend boyfriend.
He would not see me.
He did not want to see me.
So, he ended it over and over again,
because I chased him with all my heart
over and over again.

It left me broken in two.
And he knew it.

He relished it.
It's always been about him.
These past 5 years.
It's always been about him.

I just wanted someone for me
That one person
I'm still waiting.

MASS

The fear is permanently there
When he is here
Why does it linger?
I take a deep breath in.
It stays.

He'll destroy me?
He'll ruin me?
But I've been through it all and come out strong.
He is always wrong.

I am ahead. Leave him be dead.
Would it be better if he is not here?
Why can't I let it go?
Why do I feel he'll ruin me?
Fear, fear, fear.
Tears, tears, tears.
I'm fed up of the fear and tears.

I will let go. I choose to let go.
Just let go of the fear.
Did I know him in another life? He makes me feel
awkward. Why does he scare me So?
I need this miracle.
Change my thoughts.
Shift it. Peace.

YENOM

We all want it.
But nobody talks about it.
You're my one love
My big love, Baby!

"Past Let Go"

What of the past that keeps me
Stuck?

Why do you cling to me?
Why on Wye? Can't I let you go?

I surrender to you God!
Yet
You place me back in this
                    White Cube.
Driving me mad! *Are you?*
My Artistic sustenance?

Yet you never let me follow that Art
Path.
But then again I got to meet him in
Bath.

The one who made me go on.
When really I had *always* won.

LUXURY: PART 1

Poetry is a luxury.
Illustration is a luxury.
My Heart.
Your Art.

Redefining luxury.
All I need is my Shaker Hymn.
So long as S & M
does not win.
How I love
to speak in this riddle.

Who is the cat, who is the fiddle?
Beware!
The sheep that howls....
But now I'm off to bed.
Dreaming of you in my head.
Not that long ago I wanted to be dead.

But I must go on.
You must go on.
We must go on.
With Simple Living.
Plain People
Inspire,
Life in The Shire.

"STUPIDLY TALENTED"

Underrated, underground.
Beneath the rubble.
Gasping for breath.

Uh-oh.
Making yet another Comeback.
It weighs too heavy.
The pressure, the pressure.

Make it like that!
Exactly like that.
No wait.
You've just started.
The light was on Red.

Now it's on Green.
But go steady.
Start when
Y-O-U A-R-E R-E-A-D-Y.

Go at your own Pace.
This is not a Race.
There is nothing to waste unless you are in haste.
So just slow down.

LOST LOVE

I don't know when you set off.
Or was it when
I got lost?
I lost you, Love.

To fail at a Dream
is a Luxury.

To forget a Dream?
A Tragedy.

This is our Purpose in Life.
Don't let convention
stab you with a knife!

Do as you please. Be selfish.
But be generous too.

Because in this world there is
Me &
You.

So reach out, hold onto it dearly.
In your heart you see what you want
Clearly.

The Corner Turns...

As we left our teen years we sang
"Just around the river bend."
Now we're older and you're no longer here.
We laugh no more.

I miss you Designer Sofa.
And all your silly ways.
Best friends
We were.

To the fashion designer.
To the starving artist.
All of it was never meant to be.... It's Best we
not be Besties like Before. In part it was my
fault. Sorry, sorry, her fault, his fault.
Miss you, confuse you, and don't have a clue
about you.

But I'm off *that* sinking ship.
Away from that Love, that Dream. The
predestined Bohemia. Accepting it.

But I'm off, up and away.

This is a call to the colour-blind, indeed.

He said Marry Me but I said Mayer Me.
The wolf in sheep's clothing stole him up to
H*$land Street, West Glasgow. Thieving. She
belongs over there, not there.

I thought I was alone.
But not for long.

Glasgow go, go, go....
Soup Can & Partick, Glasgow.

New Life, indeed.
Off the train:
All change, all change.

Dedicated to the Great City of Glasgow.

"O sweet Virgin Mary"

You loved me as a Mother would.
You were my Mother during all those
years.
Those, hard, hard, years.

My Mother who I never saw,
The Mother who I ignored.
I'm sorry, sorry, sorry.

You are My Real Mother.
Doing all I can so I can really, really see
you.
At the Real destination.
The One that it is really all about.

But I know you will come to me.
Blessed with a Vision.
I know I will see you soon.
Maybe sooner than I'd like to think.

I hope not at 36.
Like I thought when I was 14.

I might have seen you at 24, but maybe
not. Fortunately not.

But I feel you now, I see you in my own
way.
The tears, the tears, the tears
of Joy.

The realisation.
My Mother, Our Mother, the Mother of
the World.
The Blessed Virgin Mary.

Dear Martin,

Raise your glass to the Glaswegian.
Who always gave even when he was needin'.
Don't let the tears run
Away
On my Birthday.
Smile and laugh for Lisa,
It's okay.

Eat cake, be merry, it's a
Cliché,
But Everyday in Everyway
I am with you.

Raise your glass to the Glaswegian,
Who was left lying there bleedin'.

Don't waste your time.
This day is mine.
Everyday, in Everyway I love you.
That's nothing new I bid you adieu.

So raise your glass to Martin too. ☺ x

This poem was written Friday 24th July 2015 11pm
for my cousin Lisa & family. It is about her
brother who she shares a Birthday with.

RIP Martin.

Victory

You really shouldn't ever ignore greatness.

Make me as invisible as you want but that only Magnifies the vision of me in your Mind.

I know your tricks now.
Your malicious accusations are futile. Lies were your hobby.

Stop it now.

I gave too much away. I loved and loved and gave and gave.

And that rubs you up the wrong way.

You'll be seeing more of me.
But I NEVER have to see you. None of you.
Thankfully.
Amen.

***

Acknowledgements:

Thanks Mum and Dad. After all the roller-coaster rides the three of us have been through and there were some near lethal ones too. Thanks for letting me live at home and have a base in my Hometown to bring my Writing Ambitions into existence. Without the family home I grew up in my writing could never have been birthed so soon.

www.ingramcontent.com/pod-product-compliance
Lightning Source LLC
Chambersburg PA
CBHW070803050426
42452CB00012B/2478

* 9 7 8 0 9 9 3 4 0 8 9 0 8 *